Early Praise for *Be the Lead Dog*

"These fascinating tales from the sled dog trail illustrate the universality of the principles of success—from the Iditarod to the board room. I relearned some valuable lessons reading it."

Jack Canfield, featured teacher in *The Secret*, co-author of *The Success Principles*, and co-creator of the #1 New York Times best selling *Chicken Soup for the Soul®* series

****

"Read 'Be the Lead Dog' and take it to heart! Everything is here that you need to accomplish the seemingly impossible in your life. Then go hug your own dog if you are lucky enough to have one and tell them thanks, you now get it."

Brian Tracy, best-selling author of *Psychology of Selling* and president, Brian Tracy University of Sales and Entrepreneurship

****

"I found 'Be The Lead Dog: 7 Life-Changing Lessons Taught By Sled Dogs' to be one of the most cerebral pieces of writing to come out of the world of dog mushing in recent years. Authors Liz Parrish & Barbara Schaefer do a fantastic job of breaking down the various facets of sled dog behavior and applying it to numerous real world scenarios that anyone, be it beginner musher or simple dog enthusiast, can apply to their own situations.

In a book loaded with solid, introspective material, one of my favorite parts is the section dealing with 'Transparency', where the authors carefully lay out a case for mutual honesty between dog and master. This is a firm piece of work packed with useful tips and anecdotes, which I highly recommend to dog people of all levels of experience."

Jason Barron, Professional Iditarod Musher

"Liz and Barb's 'Be The Lead Dog' rocks! Funny, inspiring, with direct no-nonsense tips for maximizing your achievement potential. The combination is entertaining and so practical you can apply them today."

Craig Duswalt, Creator, RockStar System for Success

★★

"Liz and Barb, great job with 'Be The Lead Dog!' You have captured the teachings of the sled dogs simply and directly, and illustrated them with great stories I will remember for a long time. I was mesmerized by the stories of the dogs, and it was easy to see how important their lessons are. Being open to accepting their teachings is a great step toward maximizing your life potential. I will be applying these lessons to better my own life and results."

Karen Batchelor, America's Top Personal Success
Coach for 50 Somethings,
AmazingLifeAfter50.com

★★

"I loved the stories that illustrated each lesson. After reflecting on the various thoughts shared within the manuscript by Liz and Barb, I came to the realization that many of my successes in life were actually in spite of myself and how much more successful I could have been by taking to heart the types of lessons you chose to describe. I guess that is the hard truth I came away with from reading your manuscript."

Michael Halla, IT Project Manager, Indiana University

★★

"This is a quick and easy read packed with information relevant for any dog owner, not just sled dog owners. Entertaining stories highlight each lesson and reinforce each lesson. All the information is presented in an easy-to-follow format that is absolutely suited for discovering/learning and then charting the path for one's own development for themselves and their dog/s. This book will be an indispensible part of my mushing library!"

Karen-Liane Shiba, Southern California Urban Musher

"As a former Marine, I thought I was pretty tough…that was until I was introduced to Liz & Barb! With hard-hitting tips taken directly from their experience training sled dogs, 'Be the Lead Dog' is both a practical and inspirational guide to becoming a passionate, effective leader at any level. Get this book & read it. After dog-earing the transformational strategies (pun intended), then apply them & see the difference this book makes in your relationships, your business, and your life!"

Ed Rush, Former Marine Corps F-18 Pilot, Speaker, Author, & Coach, **www.EdRush.com**

★★

"'Be the Lead Dog' contains no gimmicks—just genuine and heartfelt stories that vividly illustrate the power and value of the human-animal connection. The lessons learned are told in a way that is easy to understand and apply. Having been Liz's dog handler for the many training races and the Iditarod race, I witnessed the triumphant validation of applying the seven life changing lessons as she and the team finished strong that morning of March 17, 2008 in Nome, AK. After experiencing that, there is no doubt in my mind that what Liz and Barb convey in the book really works!!"

Elaine Gazdeck, Director of Quality Assurance/Regulatory Compliance, Array BioPharma Inc.

★★

"Truly wonderful! Once I started reading it, I found it hard to stop. The content is entertaining, inspiring, and motivating."

Mary McNally, President, Project Training Plus, LLC

★★

"'Be the Lead Dog' is a great book and is filled with stories and key takeaways that will make you and your organization more effective than ever before. Being the lead dog is truly the way to go…and Barbara and Liz will show you how to get there!"

Jonathan Sprinkles, Voted Speaker of the Year (APCA), Voted Mentor of the Year (Walt Disney Company), Voted Marketer of the Year (JMI, Inc.); **www.JonathanSprinkles.com**

"Everyone should take the information in 'Be The Lead Dog' to heart. The sled dogs speak to us all when they reveal, simply and directly, the secrets for a well-lived life and how to accomplish what you set out to do."

James Malinchak, 2-time College Speaker of the Year, co-author of *Chicken Soup for the College Soul*, founder of **BigMoneySpeaker.com**

****

"'Be The Lead Dog' provides lessons for all who lead and teach leadership. A fun and thought-provoking read."

Cathy Rush, Member of the Womens Basketball Hall of Fame, President of Future Camps, **www.cathyrush.com**

****

"All in all, I think it is a great tale of two extraordinary women and their equally extraordinary teachers. It led me to reexamine the ways I have responded to recent events in my own life. I guess you met your objective!"

Jeanie Sheehan, Fremont-Winema National Forests, USFS (Ret'd)

iv

- BE THE -
LEAD DOG

7 LIFE-CHANGING LESSONS TAUGHT BY SLED DOGS

LIZ PARRISH AND BARBARA SCHAEFER

ISBN: 978-0-9841254-1-8
Library of Congress Control Number: 2009913701

First Edition 2010
Current Printing: 1

Printed in the United States of America

Disclaimer: The purpose of this book is to educate and entertain. Neither the authors
nor publisher guarantee that anyone following the techniques, suggestions, tips, ideas or
strategies contained in this book will have any specific or definite measure of success. The
author and publisher shall have no liability or responsibility to anyone with respect to any
loss or damage caused, alleged to be caused, either directly or indirectly by the information
contained in this book.

Cover and interior design by Nu-Image Design (**www.marketingcommand.com**)

Cover dog photograph courtesy of Kippy S. Lanker, Geminai Graphics and Photography
Cover background photography courtesy of Liz Parrish

Liz Parrish author photo courtesy of Karen DeMello
Barbara Schaefer author photo courtesy of John Hart

Life Through Dogs, LLC
P.O. Box 498
Ft. Klamath, OR 97626
888-583-4121
www.LifeThroughDogs.com

This book is dedicated to all our teachers and mentors, canine and human alike, who have graced our lives with your presence, teachings and wisdom.

Our lives are immeasurably richer because of you.

Acknowledgements

One of the most fruitful applications of the Lessons in this book is the development of incredible teamwork. Every project requires teamwork of some sort, and certainly producing a book is no exception.

To the many supporters of our respective kennels, Briar's Patch Sled Dogs and Qualobo Siberians, our ongoing and extended thanks for carrying us through. It's amazing to reflect on all your support has done for us, enabling the incredible adventures we're fortunate to be able to share.

Among our many human mentors, a few have made the biggest impact. In learning to understand and implement the Lessons from the Sled Dogs, Jamie Nelson and Ann and Al Stead are the best of the best. Maureen Gundersen was Barb's first sled dog mentor and is dearly missed; she continues to be remembered as someone who touched many lives through her Siberian Huskies and Australian Cattle Dogs.

Many thanks to our business coach and mentor James Malinchak, as well as the incredible entrepreneurs we are fortunate enough to network and mastermind with as part of his program. James has given us the means and impetus to "get us off our assets" and share these incredible Lessons in a meaningful and timely way. Thank you all for your support, encouragement, and accountability.

Thanks also to Cathleen Collins, our hardworking copy editor, who has helped us fashion a rough manuscript into a finished work in very short order. Thanks for containing all those ellipses! We appreciate all the pre-publication reviews and inputs from Karen-Liane Shiba, Pat Hanson, Mike Halla, Jeanie Sheehan and Mary McNally, as well as others who read, encouraged, suggested, and commented. We got 'er done, thanks to you.

And finally — always — we are forever grateful and indebted to our amazing, marvelous, incredible teachers...our sled dogs. Each and every one has had something to teach us, and we tried hard to learn as much as we could. Humans are kind of dense sometimes, and it takes a while for your teachings to sink in. Thanks for being there for us, and being just as you are. You've taken us places — physically, emotionally, spiritually — that we could not visit otherwise.

Contents

Foreword

When reading this book for the first time, we were struck by the clarity of vision Barb and Liz displayed in discussing their work with sled dogs. They mention that dog people, "get it"; they indeed do, but very few of us are able to put what we "get" into a format that is easily understood.

Be the Lead Dog does a remarkable job in setting forth the simple tenets of being a sled dog, and what we, as trainers, can be trained to do. Dogs are very basic animals that see their life simplistically, and while we have introduced many more complications into our world, our dogs will still only see the unpretentious truths that govern all of our lives.

Zoya and I have lived and worked with sled dogs for many years, and I am convinced that we will never learn all that they have to teach us. Every day is a new day; this book will show you how to explore the possibilities.

> John Schandelmeier and Zoya DeNure
> Yukon Quest Champion and Iditarod Musher
> Crazy Dog Kennel
> Gakona, AK

Preface

Be the Lead Dog evolved as our way to capture and share the many important life-changing lessons we learned from the greatest teachers in our lives…our amazing sled dogs.

We both spent many years learning from our dogs, and they taught us far more than we taught them. All dog and human relationships have this potential, if the human member is open to the possibilities. Our relationships with our sled dogs are, by necessity, much deeper than that with your average house pet. We spent many thousands of hours working with our dogs, both individually and as a team, to accomplish our goals. Those goals range from sled dog racing, dryland training, developing individual dogs as leaders, or simply helping a dog overcome a fear or control their emotions and responses to their environment.

Often, when people first meet our dogs and learn they are sled dogs, we address a number of questions and misconceptions. The dogs are so small, how can they pull a heavy sled? Aren't they mean? Why do they live outside in a dog yard? Don't they get cold in the winter? Do they all have names? Do you know all their names? These questions are born out of media stereotypes (as a kennel visitor once remarked, having read too many Jack London stories) and lack of experience with these amazingly intuitive dogs. When you spend so many years, hours and miles working together, under all conditions, you get to know each other as intimately as two different species possibly can. That is where the magic of the sled dogs becomes apparent — *they* have been consistent in *their* teachings, but it took *us* a while to realize this and then be in a position to share these teachings with you.

Thus, our business venture of Life…Through Dogs[SM] was born. Our key tenet is that dogs mirror and reflect, with absolute clarity,

3

where we are at any given moment, and how harmoniously we are living. Life…Through Dogs offers a variety of information products, adventure experiences, and hands-on training clinics utilizing the sled dogs as our primary instructors. People engaged in our hands-on urban dog sledding on wheels clinic or undertaking our ultimate sled dog immersion adventure experience believe they are learning about how to train and run the dogs, whether ours or their own. They do — and learn about themselves in a deep and often profound way. Sometimes it is Patience, sometimes Perseverance, often it is Trust or the other Lessons in this book…folks learn the lesson they need most at that time.

Dog people "get it," because they have had the same experience with the dogs in their lives. Sled dogs (in fact, all dogs) "read your mind": dogs are happy when you are happy, sad when you are sad, know when something is up or different. There is a lot more to the dogs than meets the eye…and the dogs understand the same applies to people too.

Sled dogs react to and reflect your INTENT. Invariably they highlight an issue or problem, often one you did not realize you had. Occasionally they wow and amaze you, accomplishing the seemingly impossible — things you didn't even know they knew how to do or were capable of doing. Sometimes they simply are there for you and provide that mirror to let you know they see you exactly as you are. The observations and stories in this book illustrate how that happens, and what it can mean to you as you seek to understand and deal more effectively with others…and with yourself.

This book is not a primer on sled dogs or how to train dogs. This is about how the dogs train us — show us universal truths, and at times hard truths about ourselves and what we need to learn.

Having said that, here is a little terminology that will help you understand the stories used to illustrate the key lessons of this book.

Musher: The person who drives the team. The musher is the "top dog" — as opposed to the lead dog — and the one whom the lead dogs and the rest of the team look to for direction, confidence, support, coaching, care, and love.

Dog Team: The collection of dogs, one or more, who work together and with their musher to accomplish a goal. When they come together as a team, they understand their power and they experience accomplishing more by working together as a whole rather than as a group of individuals.

4-wheeler/ATV: 4-wheeled all-terrain vehicle, used to train dog teams when there is not enough snow to safely use a sled. ATVs (also sometimes called "quads") are terrific training tools for dog teams, because the musher has control and can teach commands, discipline, control speed, and fine tune the team. They feature locking brakes, enabling the musher to get off and work with the dogs in the team while teaching commands. Typically, the engine is on and in gear, so that the dogs have resistance and pull against the gears, thus controlling their speed and helping them develop pacing and gait.

Leaders/Lead dogs: The dog or dogs in the very front of a team. The leaders typically do the mental work and develop mental toughness to handle the pressures of their job. Lead dogs must navigate the trail, negotiate obstacles, set the pace for the team, listen for the musher's commands and execute them...all the while being chased by a big pack of dogs that is the rest of the team. The position and responsibility involves a lot of mental pressure, and we rotate the dogs out of lead into the middle of the team to give them a mental break and refresher.

Point/Swing dogs: The positions just behind lead, these dogs help the leaders in driving the team forward and around corners and obstacles. Often these are less experienced leaders that are gaining experience being up front and learning from seasoned leaders.

Team dogs: The dogs in the middle of the team are on autopilot. They don't need to think, they just go. Dogs are rotated into team to give them a rest from the other positions.

Wheel dogs: The dogs at the back of the team, who are just in front of the vehicle being pulled, they provide the steering for the ATV or sled. These dogs also provide the greatest proportion of physical work, since they are directly connected to that vehicle.

Gangline/Towline: The center line that connects all the dogs and the vehicle they tow. This line transmits the pulling power of the dogs to the sled/ATV and musher.

Commands: Voice control and directions for the team. Common commands are: "Gee" (turn right), "Haw" (turn left), "Whoa" (stop, now!), "Hike/Let's Go" (get going), "Tight/Line Out" (face forward, hold the line tight), "On-By" (keep doing what you are doing, go past a distraction or turn), and "Everybody Pull!" (extra team effort).

Use *Be the Lead Dog* for self-development as well as inspiration and entertainment. We define and describe each Lesson, then illustrate it with specific stories of how it manifests itself. Action Tips are included for applying each Lesson, and we provide a space for you to develop your own personal action plan.

Each Lesson also references additional resources on our website, **BeTheLeadDogBook.com**, where we are able to include multi-media content to complete and complement the book. Be sure to visit and take advantage of the tools and useful information available there, including quizzes, videos, audios, images and interactive documents that personalize each Lesson and bring it home to you.

The dogs take us on an experience which is a lifetime of learning… welcome to the view from the other end of the gangline!

Introduction
Sled Dogs as Teachers

We have often participated in Mushing Boot Camp, a three-day intensive hands-on seminar to teach mushers how to train their own dogs. These are typically held on the West Coast in early May, timed for cool weather and training on dirt, where the dogs either pull a 4-wheeler or cart vehicle. This dirt training is rigorous, an opportunity to perfect the dogs' discipline and execution of commands.

One day early in the training of her own team, Liz was participating with a small team of six dogs and doing open fieldwork with the instructors, Barb, and the rest of the students. Her leaders were Sinclair and Gerry; Gerry trained as a young leader the previous season, and Sinclair was just starting out. Instead of following a defined trail through woods or along the side of the road, she directed the dogs across an open field, where they would need to listen and follow directions.

In this scenario, when they got into the open field, Sinclair and Gerry were unsure of themselves and the commands of which direction to turn, so Liz stopped the team to walk up and move the leaders into the position where she was directing them. As she tried to return to her 4-wheeler, Sinclair kept turning around to watch Liz and moving back into her original position; Gerry willingly followed. Liz kept returning to the front of the team to put her in the correct position, and commanded Sinclair to "line out." Sinclair kept it up, insisting on turning to watch Liz and moving back to where they originally stopped. Liz got increasingly frustrated with Sinclair on each returning trip to correct her, and Sinclair's behavior became more entrenched. The situation escalated until the instructor finally intervened.

Several truths emerged that day: Sinclair kept getting worse the more frustrated Liz became. Liz kept doing the same thing and kept getting the same result. When she was frustrated, she lost her creativity and flexibility. Sinclair's behavior was reflecting Liz's frustration — as Liz shut down, so did Sinclair. When Liz stepped back and calmed down, so did the dogs, and things instantly improved. How many times and in how many situations has that happened in your life?

Sled dog training, especially training leaders, is all about Trust, Patience and Focus, and their auxiliary attributes: Drive, Self-Assurance, Perseverance, and Transparency. By developing those skills, we connect with the dogs on a level where we can truly communicate with them. The dogs innately have those skills, as a function of the beings that they are. We need to develop and hone our skills to a level where we can understand and be "on the same wavelength" for communication and cooperation.

Many philosophies and personal development methodologies speak of being in the moment, living life fully, etc. It is hard to understand how to do that without role models and examples. The sled dogs provide innumerable clear examples and point the way to implementing these universal truths. Therefore, we examine and study the lessons they teach for specifics on how to accomplish this in our own lives.

Focus

FOCUS: *to concentrate attention or energy; to adjust one's eye to a particular range; to render an object or image in clear outline or sharp detail by adjustment of one's vision; close or narrow attention.*

It is that concentration of attention and energy that gives Focus its power. Because we often live our lives without the sled dog level of Focus, we surprise and amaze others and ourselves when we bring that Focus to bear — we get things done, learn new skills or information, and fulfill our desires and promise.

Focus enables you, like the sled dogs, to do things that require bringing ALL of yourself to bear. Focus also has an element of how things are achieved, and the process of achievement itself. When you live with Focus, you devote yourself exclusively to what you are doing at that moment, whether it is eating dinner, closing a business deal, finishing your daily workout or changing a diaper. You are absorbed by what you are doing, and not distracted by past or future actions, thoughts, and feelings. Therefore, with Focus, you not only accomplish extraordinary results, you can also enjoy and get the most out of the most ordinary of daily activities.

Focus is a learned skill, and can be mastered, refined, and optimized with practice and feedback. Reinforcement is key. Once you are aware of your level of Focus (or lack thereof), you can devise ways to "just get it done"…and discover the joy of the "doing," as well as the sense of accomplishment when you finish tasks.

The antithesis of Focus is distraction. Distractions abound with things happening in our environment (activity, TV, noises), and also by our own minds (what's for dinner, whom to call, what bills to pay, what did that conversation mean…). The opportunities for distraction are limitless, whether in the work or personal environment. Recognize when you are getting distracted and use that recognition to refocus on the task or activity at hand.

Benefits of Focus:

The primary benefit is one of accomplishment, particularly of the unlikely or seemingly impossible (in quantity, learning, or activity). Personal fulfillment and accomplishment is achieved through focusing on each and every activity you do: doing it to the best of your ability, challenging yourself to do it faster or better, learning more from it, seeing more opportunities for results. Regardless of the results, you always have the satisfaction of knowing you did your best.

How sled dogs demonstrate Focus:

Another way of saying that sled dogs are masters of Focus is that they live in the moment. Nothing is more important to them than the here and now and what they are engaged in at that instant. They are utterly capable of enjoying pulling their load down the trail, eating the same food every meal of their lives, playing and romping like there's no tomorrow, and working together as a team to accomplish what they cannot as individuals.

Sled dogs devote themselves to what IS, and what they are doing right now. They are the poster children for undivided attention, and perform best when we give them our undivided attention as well. When we do not — when we are thinking about anything else besides what we are doing at that instant — things go bad in a hurry!

Focus Stories:

Liz: Early on in my learning to be a musher, I only had one sled dog, an older husky named Briar. My mentor had trained and raced her as a leader, and she had that intangible leadership quality whereby the team could accomplish more with her in lead than with another dog. She was an incredible first dog from which to learn the sled dog Lessons. I often brought her with me when I would travel up to Barb's place in Grass Valley to train, and put her in the team with Barb's dogs.

One afternoon we took all the dogs out for a longer training run, expecting to be out several hours because we were also stopping to teach the dogs to rest. Briar and one of Barb's dogs named Dale were in lead, both experienced leaders. We did a loop trail we had done in the past, although this time we did it clockwise, instead of the usual counter-clockwise.

Things looked a little different doing the loop backwards, and we missed a turn — what was to be a 20-mile loop turned into about a 35-mile loop. We figured out what happened, and we had a general idea of where we were, and where we needed to be, but we were on logging roads we had not trained on before. The dogs reveled in being on new trail, and thoroughly enjoyed pulling up and over the ridges as the miles added up.

Night fell, and the dogs love running at night — it is cooler for them, and the woods come alive with smells, sights, and sounds that are missing during the day. We were also prepared to be out there, with headlamps, snacks, and drinks since we had planned to stop to practice resting, so there was no danger. We just had to figure out how to get back to the main road where our dog truck was.

Briar and Dale knew that the main road and the dog truck were to our right, and they proceeded to take the team down every single right hand road intersection we came to. They were correct, except that this late in the fall, the Forest Service locked and gated the roads. Every time we reached a gate, we had to turn the long team around and head back to the road we had been on and continue. Next right hand turn, Briar and Dale took it — again, a locked gate, another turnaround.

Finally, we got back to the main road, turned right, and headed back to the truck at the bottom of the hill. Meanwhile, Barb's husband John had been worried about us when we were several hours late in returning, so he had gotten some help, found the dog truck and moved it a couple of miles further up the main road, and then set out from there to look for us. We came across John shortly after getting back on the main road, and then continued toward the dog truck. The dogs knew the truck was at the bottom of the hill, where we had started from, and so when we came around a corner mid-way down the hill and there it was, they pulled right past it, intent on reaching where they had left it. We insisted on stopping, and had to use full brakes to get them "out of the zone" so that they realized the truck was right in front of them; the run was over and they could get a well-deserved rest.

Barb: In late fall, we had a training weekend at Crystalwood Lodge (Liz's place), attended by a variety of teams, both large and small. Liz and I were training our big teams and going longer distances, and we invited Joyce, a one-dog team owner, to come and experience running with a big team. The route included a couple of miles on Liz's property, then a half-mile or so along the shoulder of the highway, to get over to many more miles of Forest Service roads and trails. As we often run on trails with other teams, it is VERY important the dogs stay on the right-hand side of the road, called "gee-over," and especially so on a road with vehicular traffic.

I'd had a discussion with Joyce ahead of time about how I'm anxious about running along the highway, and how the dogs are pretty good at reading our minds, and especially good at paying attention to what we are focused on. Therefore, Joyce needed to look at where we were headed, and where we wanted the dogs to be rather than at any distractions like passing logging trucks, cars, etc.

We got onto the road, and shortly we heard a logging truck coming up the road behind us. The dogs, almost as if in response, started veering left, out into the road lane. I quickly tapped Joyce on the knee and said, "Joyce! What are you paying attention to?!" She replied, "Oh,

I'm so sorry!" I reminded her to pay attention to where we needed to be, not where she was worried. I called out "Gee-Over," and we both concentrated on 10 feet up ahead of the dog team, on the tree that was off the right-hand shoulder. The dogs moved back over and stayed there, and the trucks safely passed us by.

The dogs taught me to focus on where I want to go. This does not mean you don't pay attention to where you are or what is happening, but you focus your energy and attention on where you want to be.

Action Tips (How to Focus like the sled dogs):

- Devise reinforcements to reward yourself for having Focus or penalize yourself for lacking Focus. Just like the dogs, you can train yourself or your team to focus through both positive and negative reinforcements.

- Time constraints and deadlines have a magical way of providing that needed motivation to Focus and get things done.

- Establish a habit of Focus. Consistency is key.

- Instead of multi-tasking, implement serial tasking. With each thing you are doing, zero in on that and that alone while you are doing it. Then move on to the next item, and grace it with that same level of focus. You will be amazed at what you do and complete.

- Acknowledge when you do get distracted, recognize what happened, and do not allow excuses to take over. There will always be the opportunity for distraction; Focus is about developing the discipline not to take the bait, until your ability to Focus is so habitual that distractions are easy to ignore.

- Turn off the distractions, even if only for short periods. Turn OFF the cell phone, shut down the email, close the door, politely excuse yourself, and do not allow yourself any excuses for not getting your task accomplished.

> **For additional important resources explaining how YOU can develop sled dog-like Focus, go to www.BeTheLeadDogBook.com/Focus. There you will find FREE tools such as a quiz and practice tips to get you on track to fine tune your Focus.**

What This Means to Me
(Focus notes/personal action plan):

_____

_____

_____

_____

_____

_____

_____

_____

_____

_____

_____

_____

_____

_____

Lesson 2
Patience

PATIENCE: *the bearing of provocation, annoyance, misfortune, or pain, without complaint, loss of temper, irritation, or the like; diligence; endurance.*

The dogs — like people — are an intriguing mixture of patience and impatience. They will seem to bear trials and tribulations to no end (bad weather, tough trails), and yet throw a fit if another dog is fed before they are. They will wait forever for their musher to return or to go for a run — but give chase the instant another team passes them.

Opportunities for patience abound for both dogs and people: Patience with your external situation, circumstances or environment, many times largely out of your control; Patience with others — often more difficult, because you must deal with others' changing reactions (here you find your own Patience will elicit a response in kind from those you deal with); and, of course the toughest one of all…Patience with yourself and your own reactions. This is where Patience yields its greatest reward — when you can show yourself kindness and compassion.

Patience is a conscious act…it does not mean becoming a doormat, or resigning yourself to everything that comes your way. The dogs teach us that balance. As mushers, we learn the difference between applying Patience to teaching a new skill/behavior versus dealing with dogs' bad behavior, as when they are acting out even though they know better. Sometimes getting mad is a good thing — not necessarily to blow up, but to focus and get the job done. Stop nagging. Get your point across. Then it is over. That, too, is an application of the lesson of Patience.

Benefits of Patience:

Practicing Patience means being willing to allow whatever is happening to unfold as it will, and let the fullness of time shape the outcome. That is why Patience is such a key enabler for the successful application of all of the life lessons. It allows you to actually BE THERE for what is happening, and see from a different perspective than the one with which you originally started.

Often we find that Patience allows us to step back and see the humor in a situation. Instead of getting frustrated with the 47th time to have to put a dog into the correct position (see Liz's story below), it really helps to see the comical nature of the situation and the dogs' apparent stubbornness. Patience itself is transformative… by tapping into that ability to lighten up (not shifting our focus, but applying it in a more productive and meaningful way), the dog magically "gets it" and the situation resolves itself. The same principle works very well in applying Patience to other life situations.

How sled dogs demonstrate Patience:

"Hope springs eternal"! Sled dogs are willing to wait forever — an unending series of now — for the reward.

Sled dog patience sometimes masquerades as stubbornness, and often as perseverance. The dogs often come across as stubborn because we find it hard to comprehend how they could try/do the same thing over and over and over…always hoping for the outcome of their choice. Patience plays itself out, whether it is waiting for a treat, getting to run, playing with a dog buddy or a trip in the truck. "It WILL happen, so I just gotta hang on…"

Likewise, Patience sometimes comes across as perseverance, yet it is different because Patience allows sled dogs to experience their world differently than ours. Many of the things that bother us simply do not bother them. They do not feel cold, pain, or fatigue the same way we do. Sled dog Patience has an element of acceptance. Many situations don't bother them because the situations are accepted with Patience

— that's the way things are, no reason to fret, worry, or struggle with it.

Patience Stories:

Liz: Because of their extreme focus, when sled dogs do something a certain way once, they figure it works that way forever. That can be either good, in the case of teaching desired behaviors, or bad, in the case of bad habits that need to be broken or variations on learned skills. In that process of teaching and learning, I am teaching them a specific skill, and always I am learning and practicing Patience.

For any given run, I put my dogs in position in the team, and expect them to stay there. Each run is different, with the dogs running beside different dogs, and changing which side of the gang line they run on. Dogs are right- or left-handed, just like people, so once I figure out what hand a certain dog is, I make sure to run them a lot on the opposite side of the gang line, so that they develop equal proficiency no matter where I place them. It is sometimes a struggle of wills, because the dog is initially more comfortable running on its preferred side. I learn to be very patient in reinforcing where I want them to be, placing them in position repeatedly until they finally accept my choice.

My greatest teacher of Patience has been a left-handed dog named Smoke, who absolutely insisted on running on the left side of the team, no matter how many times I unceremoniously placed her on the right. We developed an intricate cat-and-mouse game to see if I positively meant for her to run on the right side on this run, this time, right now…was I paying attention? Each and every run — 10…20…30 times, or more. The main thing is to do it until it sticks. Without frustration. In the moment. Focused on where you want to be, not what the dog is doing. The other lessons come into play, but the key enabler was Patience. It took three years of reinforcement before she felt I had learned Patience well enough; today she willingly runs on the right, no questions asked.

Barb: I have Siberian Huskies, and their instinctive prey drive can expose their inner hunter. Many of my dogs will attempt to chase a squirrel, mouse, or lizard that happens into their yard. Most of the time they are not very successful with that approach, but they continue to try. I had one dog, Dusty, who took a completely different approach. I had always thought of him as being kind of dumb and slow, but then I realized he was actually very clever…and infinitely Patient.

On a summer day, he would lie perfectly still in the yard, with his mouth slightly open, and wait. Not moving a muscle, he would lie there for hours, awaiting the next lizard or rodent that came his way. Then — snap! He caught more lizards than all the other dogs combined! He knew one would eventually come close enough. He was not distracted by a lizard two feet away; he knew he probably wouldn't get it if he charged. Thus, he waited, and his infinite Patience was rewarded time and again.

Action Tips (How to have Patience like the sled dogs):

- Breathe.

- Focus on determining WHAT you want to have happen before you jump into directing the outcome.

- This too shall pass. Realize the situation you find yourself in is only temporary; it will not be like this forever. So take each moment as it comes and make sure to do the very best you can in that moment, that instant. Let the others (moments) take care of themselves.

- Be creative. Can you think of a different approach that will solve the problem or resolve the impasse?

- Be flexible. Be willing to really understand what is going on. Seeing the situation a little differently often takes away the frustration and anger you may feel.

For additional important resources explaining how YOU can realize the benefits of sled dog-like Patience, go to www. BeTheLeadDogBook.com/Patience. There you will find FREE tools such as a quiz and audio guide to get you on track to develop your Patience.

What This Means to Me
(Patience notes/personal action plan):

_____

_____

_____

_____

_____

_____

_____

_____

_____

_____

_____

_____

_____

_____

Lesson 3
Trust

TRUST: *reliance on the integrity, strength, ability, surety, etc., of a person or thing; confidence; to do something without fear of consequences.*

We build and develop Trust over time, through repetition, and it can be easily compromised. Action and intent, and the congruence of the two are what the dogs react to in determining if they Trust you.

If the dogs Trust you to be in control, you must ALWAYS be in control. You cannot delegate or abdicate that control. Once violated, once that Trust is broken, you may never make it whole again. Just as when someone important to you violates or abuses the Trust you instill in them…your relationship is never quite the same afterward.

The dogs, individually and as a team, learn to Trust that you will always take care of them, and that you will never ask them to do something they cannot do. Once that level of Trust is established, it can be used judiciously to enable the team to accomplish miracles. A new environment, tough conditions, significant challenges all can be overcome because of the absolute Trust the dogs place in themselves, in each other, and in their musher.

Benefits of Trust:
Establishing Trust provides security, the ability to relax and feel safe. Security is a basic need which, when met, is no longer a concern — you can stop figuring out how to attain security, and relax.

As a team, you can depend on one another. Through Trust, you learn to be a team versus a collection of individuals…the team can accomplish more as a unit than the sum of the individual contributions.

Trust gives you the ability to apply skills and knowledge to new challenges and environments…and the teams' capability results in extraordinary accomplishment!

How sled dogs demonstrate Trust:

When dogs Trust, they demonstrate a willingness to try new things, or overcome scary things. When we put dogs in a new team or kennel, they innately Trust that many of the basics of the world as they know it still work — they will be fed, sheltered, trained, and run. That basic Trust enables them to figure out the specifics of a new situation — how and who will provide the food, attention, harness, etc. Once the dogs and people validate that Trust, the new relationships form.

You build Trust with consistency. The musher's basic rules never change…I will ALWAYS feed you. We/you must ALWAYS do a command. I am ALWAYS the boss.

As training progresses, the dog team and their musher live and work with each other through hundreds and thousands of hours and miles, under all sorts of conditions, and see the best and the worst of each other. That is where you build foundational Trust, out of the consistency of experience, relationship, and intent. Even very shy dogs learn to rely and relax: rely on the fact the rules never change, and that allows them to relax, even in new situations such as a different training or racing environment.

Likewise, when a team that has learned Trust encounters a new situation, even vastly different than what they have seen in training, they fall back on the gained Trust that their musher will not ask them to do something they cannot do. Therefore, they just do it…pull until told to stop. That foundational Trust carries them through amazing situations.

Trust Stories:

Liz: The very first year I had my team, I had nine young dogs that I was training from scratch. One of the more experienced dogs was a 3-year-old named Oslo. Oslo was your typical team/wheel dog, always willing to go but lacking the confidence to lead. In fact, Oslo was not a very confident dog at all, either with other dogs or with people. He paid attention to me because I brought his food and his harness, but if I had neither, he was not too interested in me or what I was doing. Since I did not spend any time teaching him to lead, our relationship was limited at best.

That first winter we ran out of snow early, and I did not want to stop training, so I thought up different things to teach the dogs in their dog yard. One of these was learning to jump up on their doghouses. Some dogs loved getting on their houses and lived up there; others thought they would die if their feet left the ground. Oslo was one of those dogs, and you could see the fear in his eyes and body. With nothing else to do, we worked on it daily. I bribed, coaxed, commanded, cajoled, and even physically put him on top of his house. I lured him with treats to no avail (this was the dog who would have easily won the kennel gluttony award). For days, weeks, and months we worked on it, on his fear. Finally, after three months, one day I said "Hup!" and he took the literal leap of faith…and lived! He was so very happy and proud of himself, and I gave him all sorts of praise and treats.

The truly marvelous outcome was the new relationship he and I developed out of this exercise. Oslo had worked it out in his own mind to Trust me, and once he did, I was now somebody important in his life. He relished my attention and praise. He came running when I called. It was amazing to see the change that simply breaking through the fear had made. A few years later when I placed him with a recreational team, he took another huge step, and now leads their team, with gusto and confidence, and is having the time of his life!

Barb: I am lucky enough to train from my house with our dirt training, and once I leave my house, within a few miles I have many miles of logging roads to use. We pass just a few houses along the way. One of those houses, however, has pit bulls.

One day when passing by that house, off to the side of the road was a litter of 4-5 week old pit bull puppies. As we approached, out charged the pit bull mamma, defending her litter and more than willing to mix it up with my dogs.

What to do? Stopping was not a good option, as that would ensure a confrontation. It was too late to turn around as she had already spotted us.

The only alternative was to go "on-by", and since it takes two to tango, trust that my dogs would mind their business as they'd been taught and not mix it up with this pit bull mother or pups. I really needed to trust that all these beliefs I have as core values were true.

I firmly gave the "On-By!", and my dogs just kept on going, totally ignoring the pit bull mother. She was trying hard to mix it up with the team, getting in there, grabbing at various dogs, and they pulled right on by, totally ignoring her. It really showed me to have Trust in their abilities and do what we needed to do without fear.

Action Tips (How to practice Trust like the sled dogs):

- Look for patterns and consistency of behavior, especially in the little things. Make sure your own behavior is consistent over time and with your intentions.

- Test the boundaries and corner conditions to make sure the results are consistent with your understanding of how the world works. Challenge those boundaries and conditions if they are not.

- Ask! Make sure the rules are well explained and unambiguous. This includes both formal rules and understanding "how we do things around here."

- Trust yourself. In order to do this, you need to understand and know yourself. Practice listening to your inner voice and intuition. It will not lead you astray.

- Reward yourself. When you establish Trust where very little or none was previously, celebrate. This is a praiseworthy accomplishment.

For additional important resources explaining how YOU can Trust and be trusted like the sled dogs, go to www. BeTheLeadDogBook.com/Trust. There you will find FREE tools such as a quiz and checklist to put you on track to Trust.

What This Means to Me
(Trust notes/personal action plan):

_____

_____

_____

_____

_____

_____

_____

_____

_____

_____

_____

_____

_____

_____

_____

Lesson 4
Transparency

TRANSPARENCY: *the quality or state of being transparent (free from pretense or deceit, easily detected or seen through); full, accurate, and timely disclosure of information; clearness or lucidity as to perception or understanding; freedom from indistinctness or ambiguity.*

Transparency of and with the sled dogs means both the clarity with which the dogs see us and our intent, as well as the clearness with which they reveal themselves and their intent and reaction. We are Transparent to them, and in turn, they are Transparent to us — that is what makes them such magnificent teachers.

Mushers say sled dogs are honest dogs, meaning that they work, eat, play, and live with the team exactly as who they are. If they are willing to do what it takes to make the team, they simply demonstrate that and tell us so, plain as day. Likewise, when they are joyful, upset, sad, excited, satisfied, or any other state, their emotional state is readily apparent through their body language and their actions.

As humans, we often put up walls and hide our true feelings, fears, motivations, and desires from each other, and just as often from ourselves. The magic and power of working with the dogs is that it is impossible to hide from them. We are utterly Transparent to them. It is their gift. They see us for who we are and where we are at this moment.

The dogs then double that gift by being utterly Transparent in their reactions and dealings with us. Just as we cannot hide from them, neither do they hide from each other or us. Motivations, emotions, fears, reactions all are immediately accessible. As they respond to us, they act as a mirror for us to be able to see and understand the impact of our intent, emotions, and actions on others and ourselves.

Benefits of Transparency:

Awareness is the key enabler for transformation. When we are fortunate enough to develop that awareness, change is often immediate because the need is apparent and we are open to it. Awareness and acknowledgement of one's true emotions, intent and actions, by readily and directly seeing the impact of them on another being, is a powerful first step in that change process.

Even striving for and accepting Transparency has tremendous benefits. One characteristic is honesty. Another is non-judgment — things and beings are the way they are, and you must deal with them in that context. Accepting Transparency is often hard, as we are not used to people who "tell it like it is." Often we discover things that make us uncomfortable. Yet when we accept them just as they are, without judgment, we unlock the key to dealing with people and situations, exactly as they need to be dealt with.

How sled dogs demonstrate Transparency:

When the harnesses come out, excitement erupts throughout the kennel. Pick me, PICK ME! I want to go! Now!

We as mushers learn to be as deliberate with the dogs as possible, and to be as aware of our emotions and clear on our intent as we can be at all times. One learns quickly the downside of that lack of vision or awareness. When you are worried about something — distracted by anything going on in your life or mind beyond this moment with the dogs — they notice that immediately, and you pay for it. They either start acting out and getting away with bad behavior or poor performance, or they start making their own decisions about where and how to go...all because you are not paying attention. When that happens, it usually injects a dose of reality in a hurry, and snaps your attention back to where it should be — at this moment, with the team and task in front of you. You may be needing to apply some of the other Lessons such as Focus or Self-Assurance, but it is Transparency that drives that home.

One of the benefits of spending thousands of hours and thousands of miles with your dogs is that you know them intimately — and they know you just as well, having seen you in innumerable moods, situations, and circumstances. The dogs are there from day one, essentially reading your mind through reading your body language and your emotions, but it usually takes most humans a while to catch on. However, over time, the symbiosis with the team becomes second nature, as a result of all the experiences shared together.

Transparency Stories:
Liz: My sled dog leaders do not like ambiguity or indecision. When other thoughts distract me, when I am not focused on the team, or when I am unsure of the right course of action, they will often make decisions and implement them for me. I then realize it is a wake-up call, bringing me back to here and now, to them. Hello in there!

The number of times this has happened are too numerous to mention. If I'm merely mildly distracted, the wake-up call can be mild — the team accelerating when they see a squirrel or deer, my leaders making a decision about which fork in the trail to take if I don't tell them soon enough. Occasionally the wake up call is more strident than other times. The first time I lost my team, I had foolishly stepped off the runners to reconnoiter a new trail, knowing the snow hook was just barely holding them. As I returned to the sled, I was fixated on thinking about getting back to the truck, how much farther we had to go…in short, everything except the dog team right in front of me. So they left, without me.

The other side of this transparency is a marvelous ability to rise to the occasion, to be able to accomplish feats I thought far beyond the dogs' abilities, in new situations and unique challenges. Over time, as my understanding and confidence grew, I came to believe they could read my mind. In fact, they do. If I imagine an action, they do it. I have willed them to stay out of harm's way and make the right choices when I did not have time to verbalize what they needed to do. It works. They may not know the situation…but they know me.

Barb: I mentor teenagers in dog sledding — I am really mentoring them about life using dog sledding as the vehicle to reach them. One of my rules for the teenagers or for anyone coming over to work with the dogs is that no matter what is going on at home or in their lives, when they go into the dog yard they leave all of that behind them. When they are working with the dogs, they need to be happy, clear, upbeat, focused, and patient. If they are grumpy and short-tempered, then the dogs would be grumpy and short-tempered. I was working with one young woman who, like many teenage girls, had problems getting along with her mom. I taught her to "shake her day off," literally, when she went into my laundry porch to put on her coveralls before going out to the dogs. The act of shaking her day off provided her the opportunity to leave her reaction to her problems behind and interact with the dogs using her true self.

One day this same young woman was to come over and take care of my dogs while I was out of town. Her sister drove her; they became lost and got into a huge fight, and her sister turned the car around and took her home, refusing to bring her over to my house. She had to come over and feed and care for the dogs since I was gone, so she asked her mom to bring her over, which of course then caused a big blowup between the two of them. Her mom was unhappy she had to do this, and they spent the entire trip yelling at each other.

When they got to my place, her mom stayed inside while she went out to take care of the dogs. The young girl remembered my requirement to be there for the dogs, and to "shake it off" at the door before she went out to the dog yard. She did. Her mom was amazed to observe the transformation in her daughter from just a few moments before — she was calm, patient, relaxed, happy, and loving, and the dogs reflected that back to her. Her mom was so amazed that she, too, donned a pair of coveralls, went out to the yard to be with her daughter, and they spent a good couple of hours talking and healing, and really communicating for the first time.

Action Tips (How to be Transparent like the sled dogs):

- Be continuously aware of your personal state. Then you begin to see the connection and impact you have on things that happen in your life.

- Show your emotions, with control. Just as young dogs learn to control their reactions (wait while stopped, don't chew on the gangline) you too can be there, show your emotions, without losing control or having your emotions control you. If you are happy with someone's work, it is OK to let him or her know that. If you are afraid of a situation or consequence, you need to acknowledge that fear as the first step to dealing with it and taming it, before it takes control of your life.

- In dealing with other people, focus on their motivations, why they are doing what they are doing. We all think we have such great walls erected around our true selves, and yet we are often already more transparent than we realize.

- Will yourself to be where you want to be. If you want to be happy, find something to smile about, and observe the effect that has. If you want to be confident, imagine what that feels like.

- Be honest with yourself and with others. It is OK to not be perfect, and OK for others not to be perfect either.

- Make sure you understand your place in the scheme of things. If that is not suitable to you, make your wishes known – be up front and clear about your intentions.

For additional important resources explaining how YOU can develop sled dog-like Transparency, go to www. BeTheLeadDogBook.com/Transparency. There you will find FREE tools such as a quiz and e-guide to get you on track to enhance your Transparency.

What This Means to Me
(Transparency notes/personal action plan):

_____

_____

_____

_____

_____

_____

_____

_____

_____

_____

_____

_____

_____

_____

_____

_____

_____

Lesson 5
Drive

DRIVE: *to strive vigorously toward a goal or objective; to work, play, or try wholeheartedly and with determination; an inner urge that stimulates activity or inhibition; a basic or instinctive need; a vigorous onset or onward course toward a goal or objective*

Drive is perhaps THE key mental aptitude that allows the sled dogs to accomplish miracles — miracles of perseverance, miracles of focus, miracles of trust and belief in self. Drive is indeed an inner urge, to try wholeheartedly and not take "no" for an answer.

Working with sled dogs has taught us that while dogs innately have varying amounts of Drive, you can also teach a certain amount of Drive. Reinforcing desired behavior such as Drive and rewarding the results of displaying Drive works for people as well as dogs. Try it! Try something wholeheartedly and with determination – you may just like the result!

Benefits of Drive:
Drive, ambition, desire…call it what you will, inner drive is what gets things done. Drive enables all the other lessons and skills to come into play and enables you to apply them.

Your Drive enables you to overcome temporary setbacks, because you still keep your eye on the prize, so to speak, and know that you are going to accomplish it. Therefore, this setback is merely a detour, not a failure, and you keep on going.

That also enables you to be creative and innovative in finding solutions, and learning new ways to accomplish your goal.

How sled dogs demonstrate Drive:

The same sled dog Drive kicks into gear, whether it is something as simple as having a meal or getting in the dog truck, or a big objective such as climbing a mountain or following a trail through a blizzard. When you watch the sled dogs' behavior, it becomes obvious they keep on going toward their objective of meal or mountain, and anything that comes in their way is something to be overcome, not an excuse for stopping.

Let's GO!

Drive Stories:
Liz: One of my good young leaders is a shy little girl named Coast, who made my Iditarod team as a 3-year-old, and did her fair share of leading during the race. Late in the fall a few months prior to the Iditarod, we were training in Minnesota, and undertook a long run of about 50 miles on a combination of forest trails and roads. The forest trails often had mud holes in them, typically filled with very cold water covered with a thin crust of ice this time of year. Huskies generally do not like water, and so going through cold water is not their favorite activity, which is exactly why we do it. This sort of training is hugely important to cement the discipline to persevere, to trust, and to keep going no matter what.

Coast was in the middle of the team on this particular trip, and we came upon a very long and wide mud hole, through which the team started to plow. Coast decided she was going to try to jump the mud hole, but of course, since she was hooked into the team she couldn't. She launched herself to try to avoid the water, landed in the middle of it…and screamed. She emerged three legged, with her right front arm sticking out at a very bad angle. Both her elbow and shoulder on that arm had been dislocated.

I was 20 miles out from the cabin, almost exactly in the middle of my run. I decided to continue forward and out onto the road, hoping to run into a deer hunter with a cell phone who could call for help. I knew those dislocations needed to be reduced as quickly as possible, and I dreaded the thought of losing her from the team. After the initial cry, she never even whimpered, and I got her up on my lap and attempted to carry her. I stopped a couple of times to flag down a passing hunter, and each time Coast would hobble slowly up to her spot in the team and wait to go. Each time I had to go get her and physically carry her back to the 4-wheeler. Finally some friends came to take her to the vet, and they too had to carry her to the truck, as she was not about to leave her team. (Good news, Coast healed quickly, made the Iditarod team and made it to Nome with no further problems).

Barb: Early on in our sled dog training, Liz and I trained my dogs together, before she had her own team. At that point in my career I had several show Siberians and several dogs I had trained as adults, who had no puppy training as sled dogs. Yet they loved to go, which was a great help as we were learning how to be mushers and learning how to train sled dogs.

One fall we took the dogs out for a slightly longer run than usual, a loop that went uphill, around a series of roads, and then back down to come home. The dogs were doing great, pulled well uphill, were strong in the loop, but as we started back downhill, which was quite steep, one of the dogs got tired and he just could not quite keep up with the pace the team was travelling. His name was Gambler, and he was nearly 10 years old, a show dog that at an older age had found his true passion when I discovered dog sledding.

We tried to slow down enough for him, but the hills were too steep. He was a good off-leash dog, so we disconnected him from the lines, thinking he could just follow along behind the ATV. As soon as we started to move, he ran his heart out to try to get back into his position in the team. Then his body would not allow him to keep pace and he would start falling behind again. We stopped, and again he charged up to his spot in the team, determined not to be left out. Again, the old guy could not quite keep up, but he was determined to try, and he would NOT be content following along behind. Finally, we realized the only way to get home was to carry him on our laps the rest of the way. He was none too happy about that, but that was the way it had to be. His head and his heart insisted he do his part in the team.

Action Tips (How to Drive like the sled dogs):

- Do not take "no" for an answer! Do not be deterred from your goal or objective.

- Develop a bias for accomplishments and results.

- Do not just do for the sake of being busy. Likewise, do not just plan for the sake of planning. Keep the end goal in mind and figure out the quickest way to get there.

- Be creative and innovative. Try something different. Try something else different.

- Ask for assistance or guidance. You do not have to take it, but getting another's perspective on your problem often jumpstarts the creative process and opens up new paths to accomplishing your objective.

For additional important resources explaining how YOU can Drive like the sled dog, go to www.BeTheLeadDogBook.com/ Drive. There you will find FREE tools such as a quiz and audio download to get you to enhance and apply your Drive.

What This Means to Me
(Drive notes/personal action plan):

_____

_____

_____

_____

_____

_____

_____

_____

_____

_____

_____

_____

_____

_____

_____

Lesson 6
Self-Assurance

Self-Assurance: *having or showing confidence and poise; self-confidence; composure, equanimity, imperturbability.*

One of the most important sled dog leader traits we look for is the dog's Self-Assurance. This self-confidence reflects a willingness to learn, to try, to make mistakes and keep learning until you get it right.

Without Self-Assurance, the brightest dog in the team will not use the ability to apply their knowledge, because they are not willing to make mistakes. Their talents and potential will go unrealized, because they are fearful and cannot grow and stretch. They will always be a follower unless they can learn to trust themselves and, more importantly, trust their ability to learn and do better.

Benefits of Self-Assurance:
The world does not always work as we wish or expect…guaranteed. There will always be changes, new information, and obstacles. Adaptability, the ability to go with the flow, is essential. An innate belief in self is the key enabler to unlocking that adaptability — being able to bounce not only back, but also higher and better than ever.

How sled dogs demonstrate Self-Assurance:
Sled dogs, like all dogs, want and need a clear understanding of what they need to do to be a good dog. They crave it, and respond 110% once they have it. That is the basis of their Self-Assurance: — "yes, I can do this, and I know what to do, so I am a Good Dog!"

Once they have that Self-Assurance, whether innate or developed, the sky is the limit. If they make a mistake, we tell them that it is not the right thing to do, then give them the direction to do the correct behavior — their tails wag so hard, you think they are going to fall off. "Now I got it right!"

One way that we develop that Self-Assurance is to stop and praise the dogs and team once they are doing the right behavior. Let's say the team is not pulling hard going up a hill. We slow down, concentrate on the pulling hard objective, and forget all else...we may walk up that hill, but as long as everyone is pulling hard, that is OK. Once they are pulling hard — even if just for a few feet at first — we immediately stop and praise the team, telling them clearly what great dogs they are. You can see the light bulbs go on and when we go again, they throw themselves into the task with renewed vigor.

Self-Assurance Stories:
Liz: One of the greatest tools I use to teach Self-Assurance with sled dogs is water/mud holes. As we mentioned earlier, most huskies do not like water anyway; snow is great, but they will turn themselves inside out to go around a small puddle of liquid water. That abhorrence of getting wet is what makes it a great tool for teaching "Yes I can!" and has really helped me to understand how challenges I face make me stronger as well.

In teaching my leaders to go through a water hole, I insist they do it right, which for them means going right down the middle, not cutting corners or tiptoeing around the edges. I can tell when I am going to have a battle on my hands after the first time through a given hole with a certain dog. They start looking for alternative paths the instant they spot the water. It often takes quite a bit of doing to get them to go through it correctly – getting off, wading in, putting the dogs in the middle of the water, putting them back, again and again, not going until they do it right. But the water hole victories are some of the ones that mean the most, because it's obvious the dogs feel a real sense of accomplishment (me too!).

Once the leaders bring the team through the water correctly, I lavish them with praise, and you can see them get so excited about themselves, sometimes literally Woo-woo-ing with excitement and happiness. I did it! I DID IT! Wow! Am I a good dog!

I attribute the Self-Assurance of my best leaders to what they were able to accomplish and prove to themselves with the water holes. Tie was my best Iditarod leader, in no small part due to the fact he became the best at going through the water holes, though not without some struggle. We had it out one day in a water hole, and I stuck with it until he did it exactly right. Always eager to please, and always hating to get wet, nonetheless the light bulb did turn on for him, at last. I could see he was proud of how he could bring the team through the water. He figured out that if he just went ahead and did it right, it was over and done so much more quickly. That same attitude and approach carried through to when we had slush or open water crossings in the Iditarod. He just knew he could do whatever I asked of him…and he did.

Barb: The first year I seriously trained for the Iditarod, I went to Minnesota to train with one of my mentors. She has a series of training trips around the end of October that are designed to really test the dogs, mushers, and in general take your training to the next level. I trucked out to Minnesota with my ATV, dogs, and gear, and I was ready to work hard, be challenged, and see what was in store for us.

At the start of the very first run, my ATV stalled and would not start. That is important because we use the engine to both brake and control the speed of the team, as well as to help the dogs out if needed. So I needed to decide, was I going to go ahead on these 25-mile runs/rest overnight/25-mile runs, etc. trip with a dead machine, knowing I would have to muscle our way through whatever came up? OK, I thought, it is what it is; I will just deal with it. At first, the going was easy, but then we got into some serious mud holes — mud up to my hips, pushing, pulling, mucking through it all. I told myself to just keep up as best as I could, and do what I could do.

Not too much farther, we went over a big bump and CRACK! The rack on the back of my ATV gave way, dumping all of my gear, dog food, sleeping bag, everything into the mud. OK, now what to do? It was 10 miles back to the house…well, I just strapped everything back on and crossed my fingers!

The trip was amazing because I had to have the attitude of "gee, I'm confident I can get through the next few miles, so I might as well do the next few miles." I was sure I could do the next thing, so I did that, and kept on going. No matter what was being thrown at me, if I got past the fear, was not afraid to try new things, was not afraid to grow – then I learned more about my ability and the dogs'.

Action Tips (How to have Self-Assurance like the sled dogs):

- Take inventory and make an honest assessment of what you know and what skills you possess. It is more than you realize. Trust in that assessment. If you find gaps in the knowledge or skills you need, fix them. That way you can rely on yourself to be able to react appropriately when encountering a new situation.

- Willingly accept praise and believe it. Everyone, even you, does praiseworthy things. Accept, and live it, incorporating it into your daily life.

- Praise your team, your family, and those you work with. Appreciation of efforts and accomplishments means a lot to all of us. By recognizing those efforts and accomplishments in others, you also develop them in yourself.

- Try new challenges. Do not be afraid to stretch and grow. That is how we find out that we can already do more than we thought we could.

For additional important resources explaining how YOU can develop sled dog-like Self-Assurance, go to www. BeTheLeadDogBook.com/Self-Assurance. There you will find FREE tools such as a quiz and videos to get you to quickly grow and enhance your capacity for Self-Assurance.

What This Means to Me
(Self-Assurance notes/personal action plan):

_____

_____

_____

_____

_____

_____

_____

_____

_____

_____

_____

_____

_____

_____

_____

_____

Lesson 7
Perseverance

PERSEVERANCE: *steady persistence in a course of action, a purpose, a state, etc., especially in spite of difficulties, obstacles, or discouragement; doggedness, tenacity.*

There is a reason that a synonym of Perseverance is "doggedness". For good and bad, perseverance is a seminal trait, allowing sled dogs to accomplish the seemingly impossible...or to exhibit stubbornness to try the soul of the most patient person alive.

The dogs, individually and more importantly as a team, spend most of their lives "in the zone," meaning that they know what they want, at that moment, and they apply all their energies to achieving that. One cannot talk about Perseverance in a vacuum. It means nothing without there being focus on a defined goal or objective, and without there being drive (the bias toward action and accomplishment), to provide movement toward that goal. Nevertheless, Perseverance is the fuel to get the dogs, or people, all the way TO the goal, not just being in motion toward it.

In the final analysis, it does not matter what happens — day or night, heat or cold, wind, open water, travelling with other teams, wildlife or alone — the dogs keep plugging along, no matter what. One of the most common, and most powerful, commands for the dogs is "On-By," which means "keep doing what you're doing, no matter what." Ignore distractions. Overcome obstacles. Disregard naysayers.

Bottom line: Quitting is not an option!

Benefits of Perseverance:

The most obvious benefit is the accomplishment of one's objectives. Perseverance also provides the feedback loop to solidify and enhance the other learnings. Through Perseverance, you discover and sharpen your ability to Focus, your Drive, your Self-Assurance. Your motives and abilities become Transparent, and you come to Trust in them. Perseverance ensures developing a healthy Patience muscle: strong, but not muscle bound, supple and flexible. You develop the ability to apply it in a wide variety of situations.

How sled dogs demonstrate Perseverance:

Just keep going. The dogs neither know, nor care, how many miles to the next rest, how long until the end of the race, where the other teams are, who's first, and who's last. They care about getting down the stretch of trail right in front of them, no matter what it takes. Just keep going.

By tapping into their reservoir of Perseverance, sled dogs accomplish incredible feats. Often those are feats overcoming the environmental adversities inherent in their job: plowing through snowdrifts so deep, they must pull hard to get the sled to go downhill; crossing a lake with a strong wind that is blowing the team sideways; going through slush or open water that encases the sled in ice; dealing with hot sun, and slogging through soft, punchy snow; developing the ability to follow a trail where none is visible to the human senses.

Perseverance Stories:

Liz: My mushing mentor has a favorite saying: "Dogs stall, people quit." What that means is that people will invariably use their dogs as their excuse to quit. Again, this speaks to the symbiosis of the dogs' and musher's mental state. If a dog or team hesitates, looking for affirmation that yes, they CAN accomplish the task before them, the musher sometimes interprets that as giving up. Thus the musher (who himself or herself is looking for an excuse) gives up and quits, thereby teaching the dogs that they CANNOT, when all the dogs were looking for was reassurance of their abilities. My mentor assured me I would see that all the time when I started running races. Absolutely true!

Often, if the weather is poor, trail tough, competition stiff, or musher tired, it all falls on the shoulders of the dog team: "Well, my dogs won't go. My dogs are distracted. My dogs won't eat. My dogs aren't pulling well." Remember that the dogs are merely reflecting what is going on in their musher's head. That person is looking for excuses to quit. The dogs are certainly convenient — "I quit for the sake of my dogs." They cannot face the fact they quit for themselves.

I also learned that even in the toughest conditions, the dogs are more than willing to go, if I am willing mentally and emotionally to lead them. Sometimes the burden of leadership is quite tiring, and I want just to have somebody else provide it for a bit, so I can just go along. However, there is only me…nobody to whom I can delegate that team responsibility. So when I was badly injured early in the Iditarod (on the 4th morning of the race, I was thrown from my sled and landed on the back of my snow hook, resulting in a huge hematoma in my right thigh), it never even occurred to me to quit. The injury was no different from the punchy snow or any of the other challenges of the trail. It was what it was. We just dealt with it and went on. Many well-meaning souls encouraged me to drop some dogs after that, to make it easier on myself and lighten my workload. I refused. I could not look any of the dogs in the eye, tell them they couldn't go because I was a little tired or sore.

Barb: I had been running dogs recreationally for several years when I decided to enter my first race in 1997, in Markleeville, California. I ran both 6-dog and 8-dog sprint teams, since it was important to race my Siberians and earn their sled dog titles by running and finishing these races.

As this was my first race, I had not been on snow very much, and I was nervous but on the first day, we did great. Shortly after coming out of the starting chute, there was a wicked inverted right-hand turn, almost 180 degrees. The turn was not too bad on Saturday, but it warmed up and melted during the day, then got cold overnight, and it became very icy.

When I hit that turn Sunday morning, I crashed on the ice, suffering a traumatic brain injury and near-death experience. I was knocked unconscious, although I didn't realize it at the time, so when I came to, another musher was coming by and gave me a lift to go catch my dog team. I got them untangled and we finished the race. I was experiencing blackouts, vomiting, inability to focus, ear ringing – all the classic signs of brain injury.

I was out of commission for two years while I struggled to heal. I was a mechanical engineer and I could not add, multiply, or divide. I could not walk more than 10 feet without passing out. My major therapy consisted of taking care of my dogs. I would not let anyone help me, I insisted on doing it all myself. I would put a chair every 10 feet throughout my house and dog yard, and sometimes it would take me all day to do the dogs, but I took care of them, and in that way started healing. They were responsible for a major part of my healing and for giving me the tenacity to figure out how to get through this and make it happen.

Action Tips (How to practice Perseverance like the sled dogs):

• Understand and believe that obstacles are temporary. The obstacle may be a sales objection, problem at work, poor grade on a school assignment, or family argument. Realize it is transient, merely a sign that you need to do something different or more to accomplish your goal.

• Do not entertain any thoughts of quitting. Shove them out of your mind immediately should they arise. Use any self-doubt or temptation to quit or change course as a signal to redouble your efforts.

• "This too shall pass." Even when dealing with situations like chronic illness or catastrophic loss, realize that some moments are lighter and better than others. Do not worry about any other moments except the one you are in right now. This one is manageable, and it is the only moment you need to address. Get through it, and it will give you the strength to get through the next one.

• As you develop your ability to apply the other Lessons, bring them back around to understand how they develop and enhance your ability to Persevere. And vice-versa: as your ability to Persevere develops, you will recognize and appreciate how that enhances your capabilities with the other skills. After all, you will have many chances to practice!

For additional important resources explaining how YOU can develop sled dog-like Perseverance, go to www. BeTheLeadDogBook.com/Perseverance. There you will find FREE tools such as a quiz and application stories to get you to quickly and easily improve your Perseverence.

What This Means to Me
(Perseverance notes/personal action plan):

_____

_____

_____

_____

_____

_____

_____

_____

_____

_____

_____

_____

_____

_____

_____

Next Steps:
Enhancing Your Life by Applying the Sled Dog Lessons

As you reflect upon the lessons from the sled dogs, we hope that you begin to see the many ways, large and small, to apply them in every life situation. Sometimes it takes thought to see how a situation would have a different outcome if you were to apply these lessons. Other times it is an intuitive recognition, a gut feeling, an "aha". The next step is proactively keeping these lessons in your toolbox to deal with situations when and as they develop. The ultimate goal is to just BE the lessons, to call upon and implement them when, where, and as they are needed. That is when you BECOME the Lead Dog.

If the stories illustrating these lessons have entertained you, we have accomplished at least that part of our goal. The dogs never take themselves too seriously, applying themselves as needed but also knowing when to relax and let go. They are funny, and life is funny. If you can see the humor in most any situation, it is automatically easier to deal with. Our hope is that the stories stick with you, inspire you, and challenge you. We leave you now with two examples that bring everything together, and show what amazing accomplishments are within your reach. Be well and Happy Trails!

Liz: One of the most potentially challenging sections of the Iditarod Trail is nearly at the end of the race, a stretch of beach trail known as the Solomon Blowhole. Teams are heading north along the beach, about 50 miles outside of Nome, and the wind blows east-to-west, from land to sea. The hills in that area funnel the wind, so teams are effectively crossing a five-mile long wind tunnel. When I got to the White Mountain checkpoint, about 77 miles from Nome, we had reports that the Blowhole was particularly bad, and as a rookie I could hardly imagine what was ahead. The race official, Joe May, gave us some cogent advice: You should travel together through the Blowhole, and you will be fine. You will not be able to see your dogs or trail markers, but that is OK — just look down at your feet and you will see the scratch marks in the snow from previous teams, and that is how you will know if you are still on the trail. The wind will be blowing right to left, so if the dogs go off-course, they will turn left (away from the wind), and you will need to get them to "gee" over to get back on the trail. You will also need to stop and "clean the windshield" periodically — wipe the accumulated ice and snow off the right side of their eyes, nose, lips, head, etc. Well, OK! No problem!

Deb Bicknell and I left White Mountain together that evening, knowing that my team was faster than Deb's, but we agreed I would wait for her before going into the Blowhole. My team went ahead, up and over the Topkok Hills, into a beautiful, clear, and still night. As we dropped out of the hills and onto the beach, the wind picked up. We stopped outside the shelter cabin before the Blowhole, and waited there about 45 minutes for Deb. I put my strongest leaders up front, Tie and Sinclair. I checked everyone's booties, checked and double-checked my headlamps. Finally, I spotted Deb's light making its way along the trail down the hills, and when she pulled up I was ready to go, as the dogs and I were tired of standing around in 20-25 mph winds. Deb announced she was not going, and that she wasn't prepared to go through the Blowhole at night. So off we went — me and 14 of my best friends to face…???

It was obvious when we entered the Blowhole. Winds that had been merely strong reached hurricane force. All the snow in the world seemed to be in the air, in motion and pounding against us. I could not see a thing beyond the butts of my wheel dogs — no dog team, no trail, no markers, nothing. I thought that, with the noise, it must be like what it is inside a washing machine. Shortly into the Blowhole, I stopped to clean the windshield, checking each dog's mental as well as physical condition as I went through the team. They were game for this, and were going without hesitation. For a split second, I realized I would be in a world of hurt if they decided not to go. As soon as the thought materialized, I put it out of my mind, and went back to relying on my confidence in them. They had done so much; I believed we could do this too, even though conditions were far worse than any in which we had ever trained. They knew how to pull until told to stop.

And pull they did. Literally into the throat of the storm, heads down, never questioning. I felt as if I was balancing on a knife's edge between terror and an incredibly intense experience, just barely on the intensity side of the balance. As the minutes and miles ticked by, my pride in my team knew no bounds. I marveled in them, their abilities, their acceptance, and was so honored to have shared the experience with them. Focus, Drive, Perseverance, Trust, Self-Assurance, Transparency, Patience. It took it all, for them and for me.

Barb: In 2006, I started training in earnest for the Iditarod. I went to Minnesota to train with my mentors, did all training events and miles, and my dogs were doing great. We returned to California and I entered my first distance race, of 135-miles, at Mt. Shasta. The midway checkpoint was at 75 miles, where my dogs would not rest (because we had not practiced it), so I ended up staying there a bit longer than planned, trying to enforce the rest, if even for a few minutes. Everyone else left, and finally I did, and headed back toward the finish line. As I got closer and closer to the finish line, my leaders would not lead. I tried all sorts of different leader combinations, but whoever was in front would screw around — sniff, pee, just not lead. The problem got worse the closer to the finish line the team got. Dogs back in the team would pull fine, but whenever I put them in lead, they would not go.

So our progress became painfully slow. Miles of patiently walking up front, getting the leaders to line out, walking back to the sled, going a couple of steps, then the leaders would not lead/go, so we'd have to do it all over again. I was going to finish, but I was not sure when. I was stressed because my husband John said he absolutely had to be back to work the next day. On the previous Tuesday John had been diagnosed with stage IV throat cancer and we had made the decision to come to the race, not tell anyone about the diagnosis, just continue with life until his treatments started. However, he had to be back to work to get things wrapped up before he started undergoing chemo.

Finally, the dogs went a few feet on their own, so I stopped and rested them. A short while later, John arrived on a snowmobile, looking for me. He said not to worry about having to quit, he could take tomorrow off. I told him I knew we were going to finish these last 10 miles, no matter what, and to go back and tell the race officials. When I finally finished about 6:30 that evening, 10 hours behind the last team, everyone other than John was at the race banquet. All I wanted to do was take care of my dogs, take a shower and sleep, but John informed me I had to go to the banquet. Very reluctantly, I did, and discovered that by finishing my race, I had provided inspiration to others, and everybody celebrated our accomplishment. When the race marshal asked me how everything went, I replied "Great! Best time I've ever had with my dogs! I can't figure out what happened with my leaders, we had done all our training and everybody else was pulling, but we got the job done!" I got the Most Perseverance Award…recognizing that it is not what happens to you, but rather how you react – not blaming my dogs, or whining, but just dealing with it for what it was.

After the race, I told this story many times, and always ended it with wondering why the dogs had the trouble they did that day. A short time later, when I told the story to one of my mentors in Minnesota, she very quietly replied, "It didn't have anything to do with the dogs." Her comment did not register with me, so I kept on retelling the story and continuing to wonder what had happened to my well-trained dog team that day.

Life went on, and John and I started his chemo, and against all odds, he survived and is now cancer-free. About a year later, when telling the race story again, I finally got the main lesson: the dogs realized I was not being truthful with myself. I had sucked it up and did the race; I had put aside my fears about John's cancer diagnosis and the possible outcome. On the outside, I was nonchalant about the diagnosis; inside I was deeply afraid. The closer and closer we came to the finish line, the closer I came to having to deal with the reality of John's diagnosis. So even though I had not been able to face my fears, or even realize them, the dogs knew. All of the lessons came into play that day, but the lesson of Transparency, of them knowing me better than I knew myself, was incredibly powerful.

About the Authors

Liz Parrish grew up in the Midwest. She attended Rice University in Texas as an electrical engineering and computer science major and then began a high tech career in California's Silicon Valley. After 21 years in a number of start-up and large corporate positions, she moved to southern Oregon and bought Crystalwood Lodge at the base of the Cascades near Klamath Falls, turning it into a pet-friendly destination resort (**www.CrystalwoodLodge.com**).

Along the way, she met and conquered challenges from childhood cancer (Wilm's tumor), meningitis, fibromyalgia, and a blood clotting disorder. The cancer treatments left her with a significantly compromised spine that has both been a challenge to her active lifestyle and an incredible source of strength.

Liz has always had a passion for dogs, dog training, and learning from these amazing teachers. She grew up with a miniature dachshund, got a cocker spaniel as soon as she could talk her roommates into it after college, and then became smitten with working dogs with her Australian shepherd, Jake. Jake never met a job he didn't like, and they tried just about everything together — agility, flyball, herding, search-and-rescue, and finally skijoring and dog sledding. When the opportunity presented itself to participate in the first ever "Mushing Boot Camp", Liz jumped at the chance. Thus, she created her first sled dog team out of her motley crew of house pets: an Australian Shepherd, a Norwegian Elkhound, and a Beagle Mix

That first of many Mushing Boot Camps was memorable for many reasons. She met her future mushing mentor, Jamie Nelson, who would shape and guide Liz's dream to run the Iditarod. She became totally hooked on the challenges and goals of training a set of dogs to accomplish something as a team. In addition, she met many lifelong friends, among them her mushing buddy and business partner, Barb Schaefer.

From that start, she spent a decade building and training her own sled dog team towards a goal of completing the 2008 Iditarod in celebration of her 50th birthday. In preparing to run the Iditarod, Liz completed a number of other races, including the Eagle Cap 200 in Joseph, Oregon, Montana's Race to the Sky, and the Siskiyou Sled Dog Race at Mt. Shasta California, as well as the Klondike 300 and Goose Bay 120 in Alaska. Liz and her team finished the 2008 Iditarod in 14 days with 14 dogs, an extraordinary achievement for a rookie — this in spite of being seriously injured early in the race and being "Iditarod's Littlest Musher."

Liz spent a lifetime preparing for the challenge of the Iditarod, and she lives by the motto, "Quitting is NOT an option."

One cannot go through an experience like the Iditarod without having it change you. Upon returning to the "real world," Liz was determined to find her new path and what life held for her, post-Iditarod. This book is one small step along that path.

★★★★★

A public speaker, an author and a leadership coach, Barbara Schaefer is also a respected teen development mentor and is known nationally and internationally for her work is this area. Barbara holds a B.S. degree in Mechanical Engineering (with an emphasis in Alternative Energy) from The University of California, Davis CA.

Barb has always been interested in animals. As a young girl, she wanted to be a veterinarian so she could work with dogs. As a teenager, she realized she wanted to be an engineer so she could make good money and play with her own dogs.

One day she was up in Markleeville and saw a woman with a 6-dog team, Barb knew what she wanted to do — dog sledding!

Siberian Husky Sled Dogs are her passion — and has been for over 20 years. Barbara and her dogs have been featured on Discovery Channel's Animal Planet, Comcast's Profiles and PBS's Central

California Chronicles. She raised and trained Jasmine who played the lead dog in Disney's *Eight Below*. Barbara is a 10-year Iditarod Sled Dog Trail volunteer, which has provided her with invaluable "insider secrets" into the relationships between sled dogs and their mushers and how that can relate to every day life.

Today, as co-owner of Life…Through Dogs, Barbara understands and communicates with both dogs and people and is able to translate these lessons into real-world practical applications — she teaches people how to "Be The Lead Dog" in their own personal and corporate lives.

Barb and her dogs earned numerous awards including:

- Siberian Husky Club of America Working/Showing Trophy in 2000, 2001, and 2002, awarded for the best multi-purpose team. Barb is only the second person to win this award for three consecutive years.

- Siberian Husky Club of America Lombard Norris Award in 2001 & 2005, awarded for the best all-Siberian Husky sled dog team.

- International Sled Dog Racing Association Gold Medals in 2002 & 2005 and Silver Medal in 2003 in the 6-dog to Unlimited Mid-distance class running all AKC Siberian Husky teams.

One of Barb's dogs, CH Fraka's Sparkl'n Jewel O'Kossok, a top winning show dog in 1994 & 1995, was awarded Best of Opposite Sex at the '94 Siberian Husky Club of America National Specialty Show and was featured in Life Magazine.

Barbara resides with her husband and kennel of 20 Siberian Huskies in the Northern California foothills of the Sierra Nevada Mountains, dividing her time between speeches, seminars and her work as a leadership coach.

More information about Liz and Barb can be found at their website, **www.LifeThroughDogs.com**.

Further Opportunities
And A FREE Gift

As John and Zoya mentioned in the foreword of this book, we will never finish learning everything the dogs have to teach. For us, that is a continual source of wonder, education, and pure joy. While the dogs are simple beings, they are mirroring the behavior, intent and actions of beings which are infinitely complex…you and I. You can easily spend the rest of your life looking into that mirror, trying to understand the nuances and changes of the reflections you find there.

Take Advantage of our FREE gift to YOU!

We hope you will take this opportunity and challenge to learn more. Because you have taken the time to read this book, we have follow-on material and a FREE gift which you are entitled to receive, to help you continue along this path of self-discovery. You can claim your free gift at **www.BeTheLeadDogBook.com/Gift**.

We realize most of our readers do not have the luxury of having their own sled dog team to provide the constant feedback and support we have discussed in the Lessons. Your challenge is to find out how to gain that same type of feedback while not forgetting or losing sight of the key messages at the core of each Lesson. That's why we put together our FREE gift to you, our reader. We want to support you as you take this information from *Be the Lead Dog* and apply it to your own challenges and life situations.

We also provide a number of ways to further engage with this material… and accelerate your process of maximizing the potential of your life. Our continuing education programs offer the perfect opportunity to work directly with Liz and/or Barb to bring the Lessons to life for you and your group or organization in an impactful and meaningful way. Life…Through Dogs also offers a variety of hands-on experiences with the dogs, either your own or utilizing our trained sled dogs, depending on what your objectives are. No matter whether you're looking for specific skills development or experience directly with the dogs, you wish to fast-track securing the benefits of implementing the Lessons in your own life and team, or are simply looking for inspiration and motivation, we have a program to meet your needs.

Continuing Education: New Programs Available
If you or others might benefit from more detail on and application of the Lessons from the Sled Dogs, we can share and elaborate on those in a variety of ways. We have presentations available for various sized groups interested in this innovative approach to learning about leadership, teambuilding, communications and overcoming adversity. Information about all these opportunities and more can be found at **www.LifeThroughDogs.com/Programs**.

Liz and Barb are available for keynote and breakout session presentations on any of the Lessons in *Be the Lead Dog*, and in particular applying those lessons to leadership, teambuilding, communications and adversity challenges in corporate, non-profit, college and youth environments. Whether you are looking for an inspiring and motivational presentation to set the stage for or wrap up a successful event, or wish to have your group delve into the benefits of implementing these lessons, we can provide exactly what you need. We are happy to partner with you or your organization to tailor our offerings to what your group needs.

Our presentations and seminars can be implemented with or without participation with the dogs, depending on your group's needs and desires. We often find that bringing the dogs into the learning environment accelerates the process, solidifies the learnings and makes them stick, just as we've described here in the book. The dogs are non-threatening and non-judgmental, and often allow people to take risks and experiment with them, whereas fear holds those same people back from trying new behaviors or risk taking when interacting with their own colleagues. If utilizing the dogs is not desired or practical, we are adept at bringing their teachings and helping our audience apply those and gain the benefits as effectively as possible.

Leadership seminars can be configured from a 45-90 minute keynote up to a two day intensive. Keynotes provide an overview of the leadership components, process and results, utilizing the Lessons from the sled dogs and liberally illustrated with stories and examples which the audience will remember and apply. The longer seminars focus on developing the leadership skills and acumen of the participants, no matter their individual leadership experience. The Lessons are equally applicable to new team leaders and senior executives, and we utilize the same training techniques as with the dogs to achieve breakthrough results with our seminar participants.

Teambuilding seminars can be done with intact teams of half day to three days duration. We work effectively with new or established teams, and go through a self-assessment to determine where the team is and what they need to focus on, then work interactively on skills development and implementation of the Lessons within the team. We can put your team on the fast track to competing in and winning whatever challenges they face.

Communications seminars and presentations can range from a 45-90 minute keynote to a half or full day intensive, depending on size of group and group needs. Communications is such a key skill in any endeavor that we utilize and apply the Lessons to develop a clear understanding and implementation of an effective communication strategy and skillset. For individuals or teams wishing to develop and excel at their communication skills there is no more effective way than to utilize the Lessons from the Sled Dogs to demonstrate and instruct on effective communication styles and behaviors.

Finally, we also provide motivational, inspirational keynotes liberally illustrated with images and stories from the trails leading to sled dog, business and life successes.

If you know of a group, school, company or organization who would like to benefit from the Lessons in this book, bulk book order discounts are available in addition to the continuing education programs. See the form on page 69 for ordering single or quantity copies of the book and material.

Hands-On Programs With the Dogs

Urban **GO** Dogs^{SM} is a hands-on urban-dog-sledding-on-wheels clinic where we teach urban mushers how to engage with the exciting and fun sport of dryland mushing. Attendees use their own dogs — of practically any breed — and learn how to easily and safely train them for dog powered travel by scooter, bicycle, cart or even skates. It's also a great way to give your urban dog a constructive outlet for their energies, help them stay in shape, and provide a wonderful bonding experience. Sign up at **www. UrbanGoDogs.com**.

Urban **GO** Dogs is currently scheduled in various locations throughout the West Coast of the United States, and Liz and Barb come to your community to hold the seminar so you can attend with minimal travel and hassle. The in-person format is an intimate setting of up to 8 teams, ensuring each team gets lots of individual attention and one-on-one instruction. The full-day seminar touches on all aspects of the training fundamentals for urban-dog-sledding-on-wheels, so you see and do exactly what you need to learn and enjoy dog powered travel in an urban setting.

Urban **GO** Dogs is also available as a self-paced home study course to allow everyone anywhere the opportunity to have fun with their urban sled dogs! The home study course includes an action guide and multi-media materials taking you through each step and topic of the in-person course, so you can learn and review with your dog on your own schedule and pace, practicing and reinforcing as necessary.

Every Urban **GO** Dogs course, whether the in-person version or the self-paced home study variety, includes our ongoing coaching support through our exclusive Trainers Inner Circle program. Ongoing monthly support includes live teleconference calls where you can get your questions answered, a monthly newsletter, opportunities for discounts and previews of new products, and private telephone consultations where Barb and Liz work with you to help you address your concerns and maximize your and your dog's enjoyment of working in harness.

For those students of the Lessons from the Sled Dogs who really want to try their hand at the full sled dog team adventure, we provide the opportunity to truly experience the magic of running a trained dog team in a wilderness setting. Run Your Own Iditarod[SM] uses our trained sled dogs, and participants spend several days bonding with, caring for and running their assigned team, under our careful supervision. The culmination of this immersion experience is a multi-stage excursion, where you get the opportunity to put it all together, utilizing all you've learned about the dogs, and yourself, to make this the trip of your lifetime. More information at **www.RunYourOwnIditarod.com**.

For more information, please contact Liz or Barb at:

Life…Through Dogs
P.O. Box 498
Ft. Klamath, OR 97626
Toll-free: 888-583-4121
Fax: 866-294-4213
Email: **contact@LifeThroughDogs.com**
www.LifeThroughDogs.com

As a reader of this book, you are entitled to **quantity discounts** on further copies of books published by Life…Through Dogs

Be the Lead Dog : *7 Life-Changing Lessons Taught by Sled Dogs* (Retail $14.95)

Practical and entertaining guide to the strategies to use to maximize your potential in Leadership, Teambuilding, Communications, and Life!

Qty.	Your Prc/Bk	Total
10	13	130
20	12	240
50	11	550
100	9	900
300	6	1800

We are interested in ordering _____ (Qty) of this book.

Print/Type Name _____ _____

Signature _____ _____

Be the Lead Dog (CD Audio Book) (Retail $21.95)
The complete text plus bonus material, read by the authors

Qty.	Your Prc/Bk	Total
10	18	180
20	16	320
50	15	750
100	12	1200
300	9	2700

We are interested in ordering _____ (Qty) of this album.

Print/Type Name _____

Signature _____

Crimp! On-By!! The True Story of a Most Unlikely Iditarod Lead Dog
(Retail $12.95)

The inspiring TRUE story of the husky named for the crimp in his nose when severely injured as a pup and relegated to being a pet...except he knew his true destiny! His unshakable belief in himself enabled him to overcome numerous challenges to lead Liz's team at the start of Iditarod 2008. An incredible motivational tale for kids of all ages.

Qty.	Your Prc/Bk	Total
10	12.5	125
20	11	220
50	10.5	525
100	9	900
300	7.5	2250

We are interested in ordering _____ (Qty) of this book.

Print/Type Name _____

Signature _____

Shipping is extra, unless we can bring the books to a presentation or speaking engagement for your group or event. To place an order, please call Life...Through Dogs at 1-888-583-4121, email **contact@lifethroughdogs.com,** or fax 1-866-294-4213.

5 Reasons to Bulk Order Books

1. **RAISE MONEY** Utilize the books in your fundraising efforts. Sell the books at your events for the retail price.

2. **REWARD** those who have helped your group by giving them a FREE autographed book.

3. **INCREASE ATTENDANCE** at your events by advertising that the first ___ people who attend will receive an autographed book. Or give away copies as **DOOR PRIZES**.

4. **RECEIVE A LOWER PRICE** than what the books would sell for at an event or through the website.

5. **BOOK SIGNING**. Have Liz or Barb keynote your event, hold a training for your group or provide books after the event, which will increase your attendance.

★★★**IDEA:** If you're having a paid admission or registration fee for your event, have the book included in all registration packets. Add the cost of the book to the registration fee so there is NO OUT OF POCKET BOOK EXPENSE for your group.